OCEAN DREAMING

A Colouring Book
for relaxation and rejuvenation

Cassie Haywood

Copyright © Soul Spirit Enterprises 2015

ISBN: 978-0-9944431-4-4

A CIP record for this book is available from the National Library of Australia

OCEAN DREAMING

In our lives we are continually bombarded with sensory stimuli, whether from our myriad of electronic devices, busy homes or the chaotic city streets. Our brains need downtime, but unfortunately we seldom get enough of it. We can always turn to water for a sense of calm and clarity. Being around the ocean gives our brain and our senses a rest from overstimulation and allows us to simply 'be'. The ocean induces a mild meditative state of calm focus and gentle awareness.

In this book you will find 30 illustrations inspired by the ocean. Simply choose an illustration which appeals to you, take a few deep breaths and start colouring. There are no rules to follow, you choose the medium and colours which speak to you. These illustrations open the way for letting go and inner peace, therefore allowing relaxation and rejuvenation to become part of your everyday life.

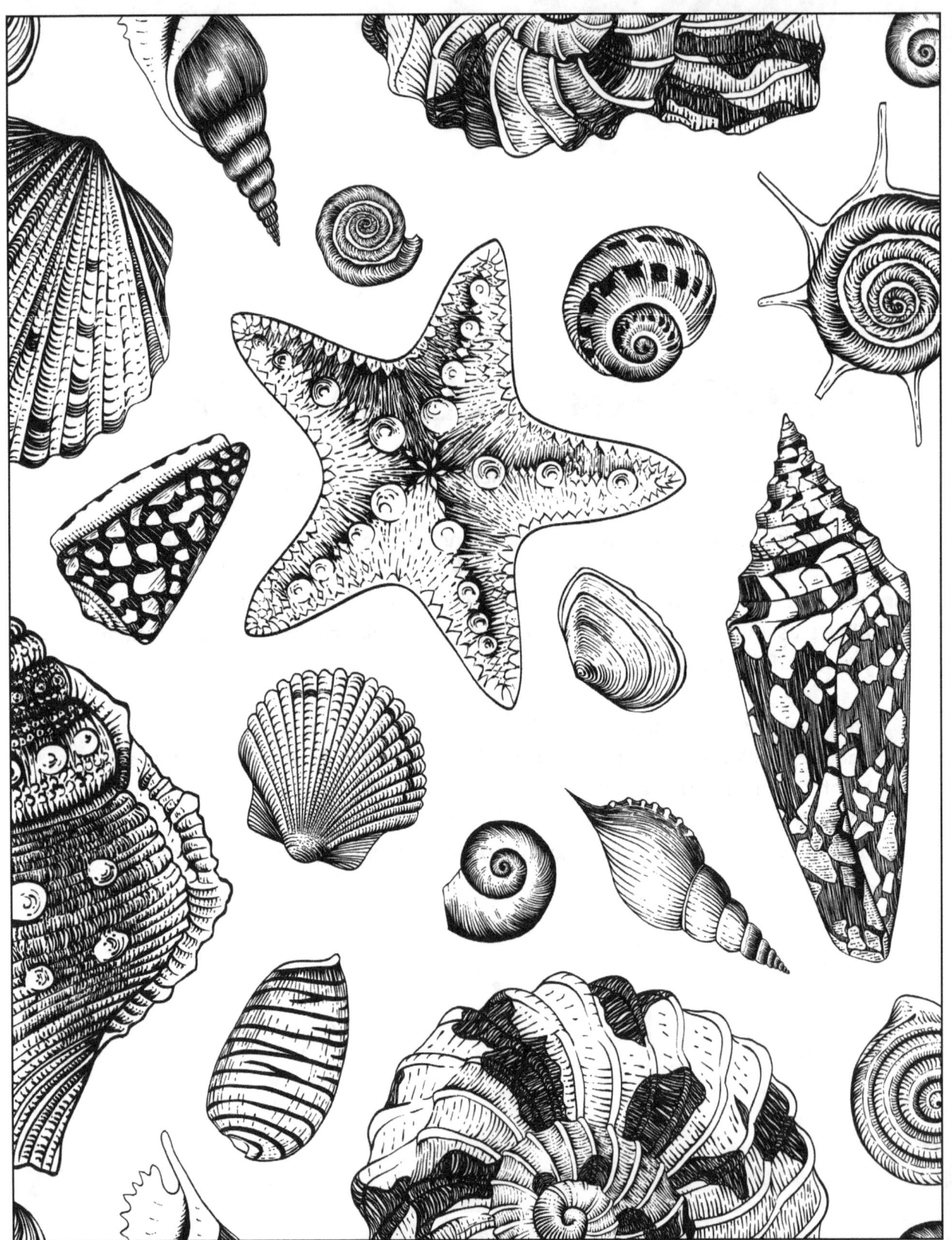

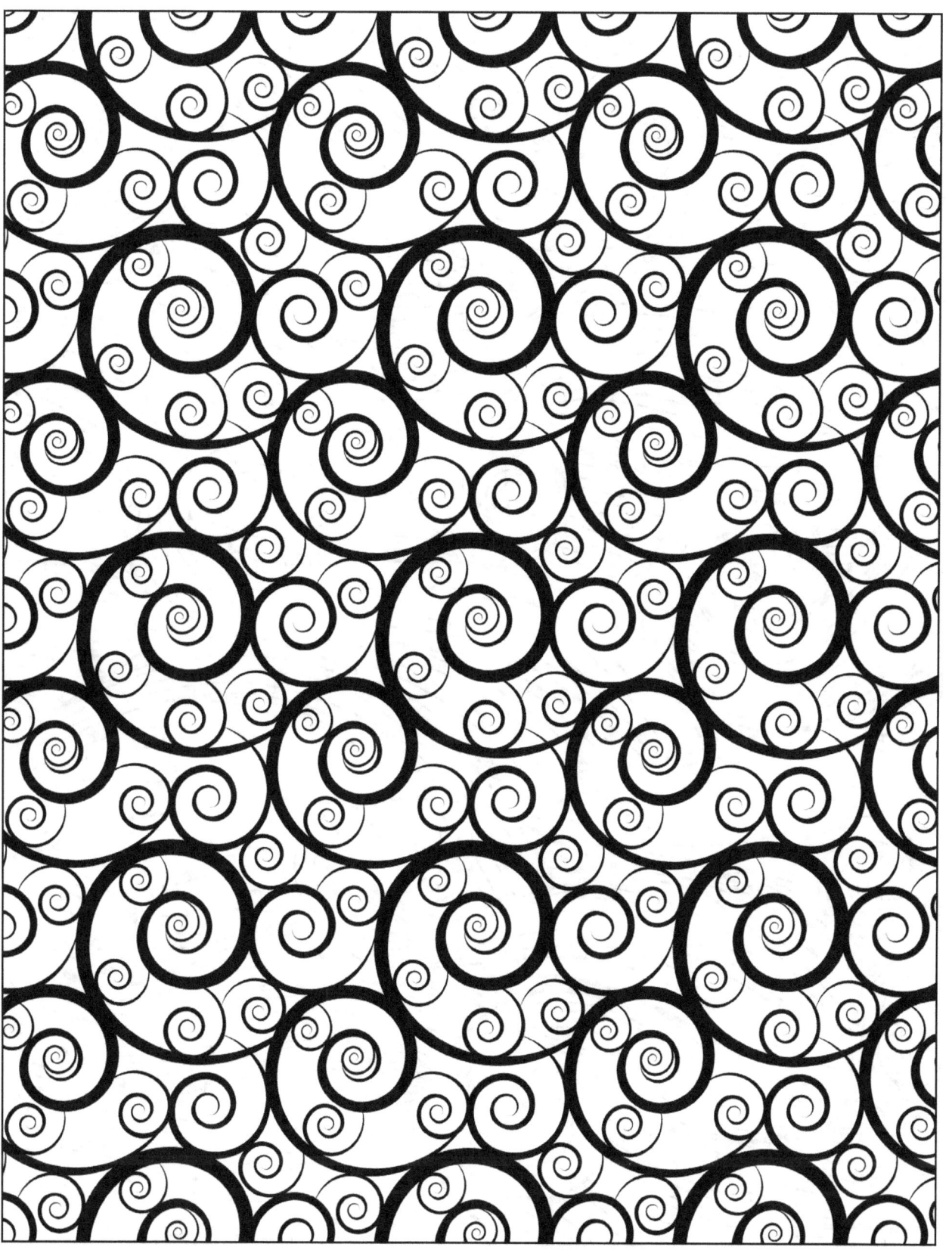

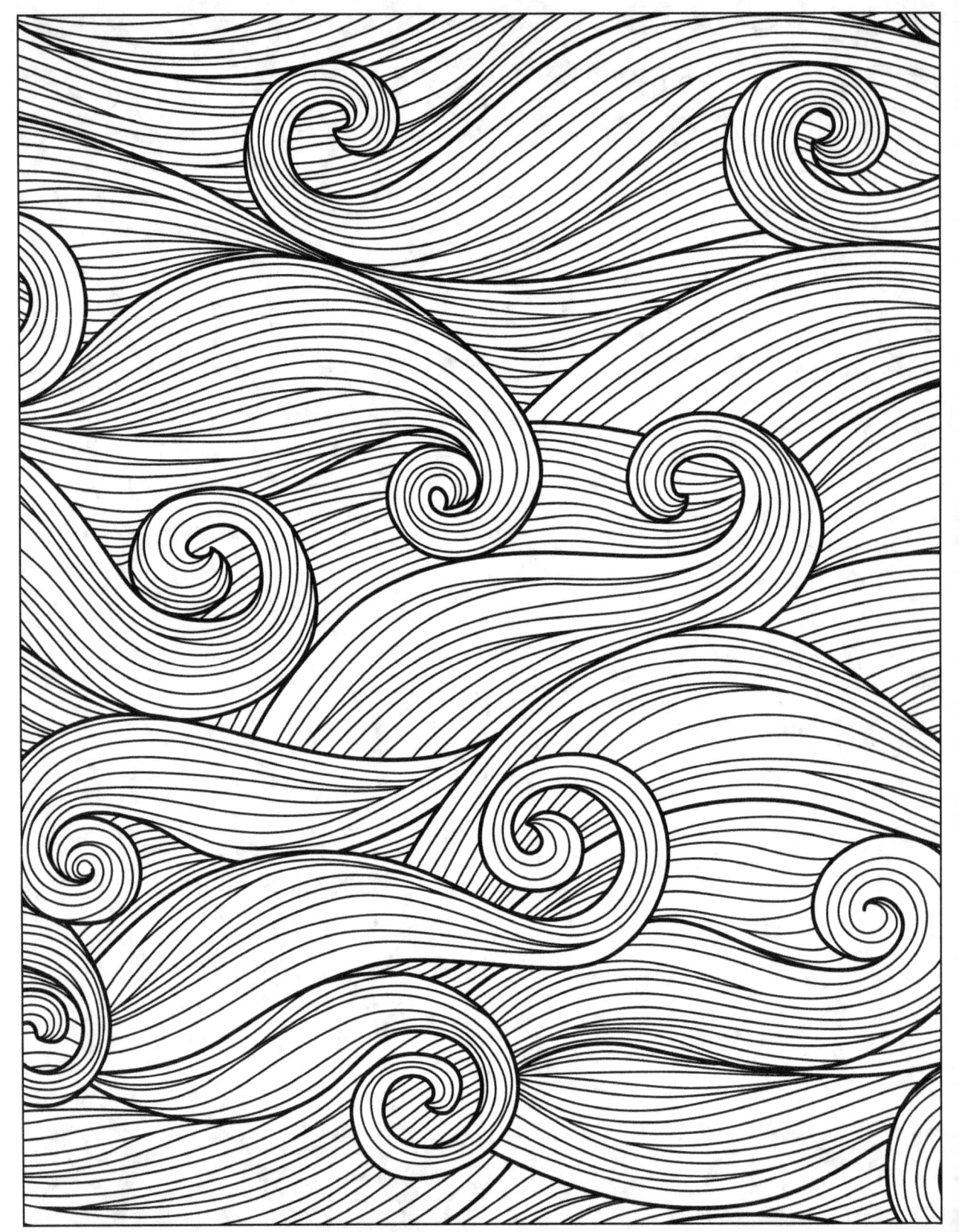

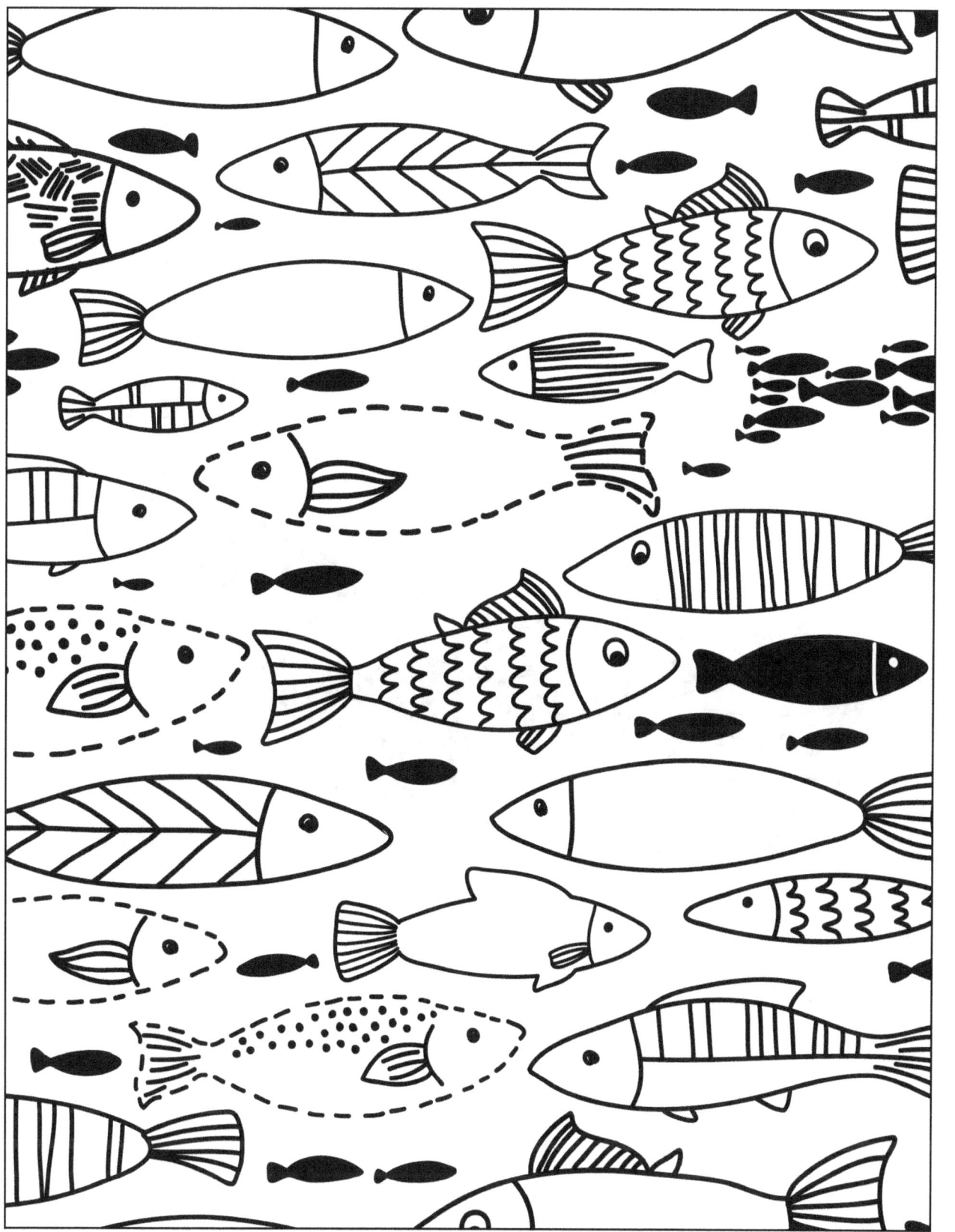

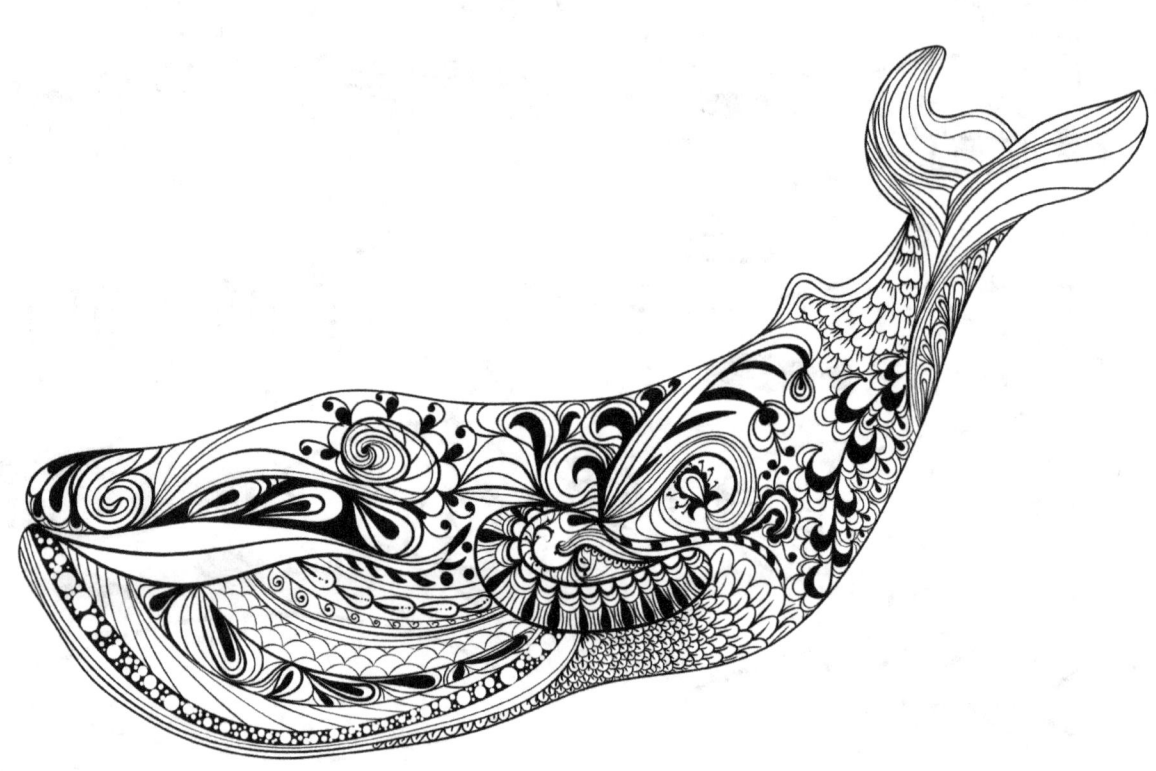

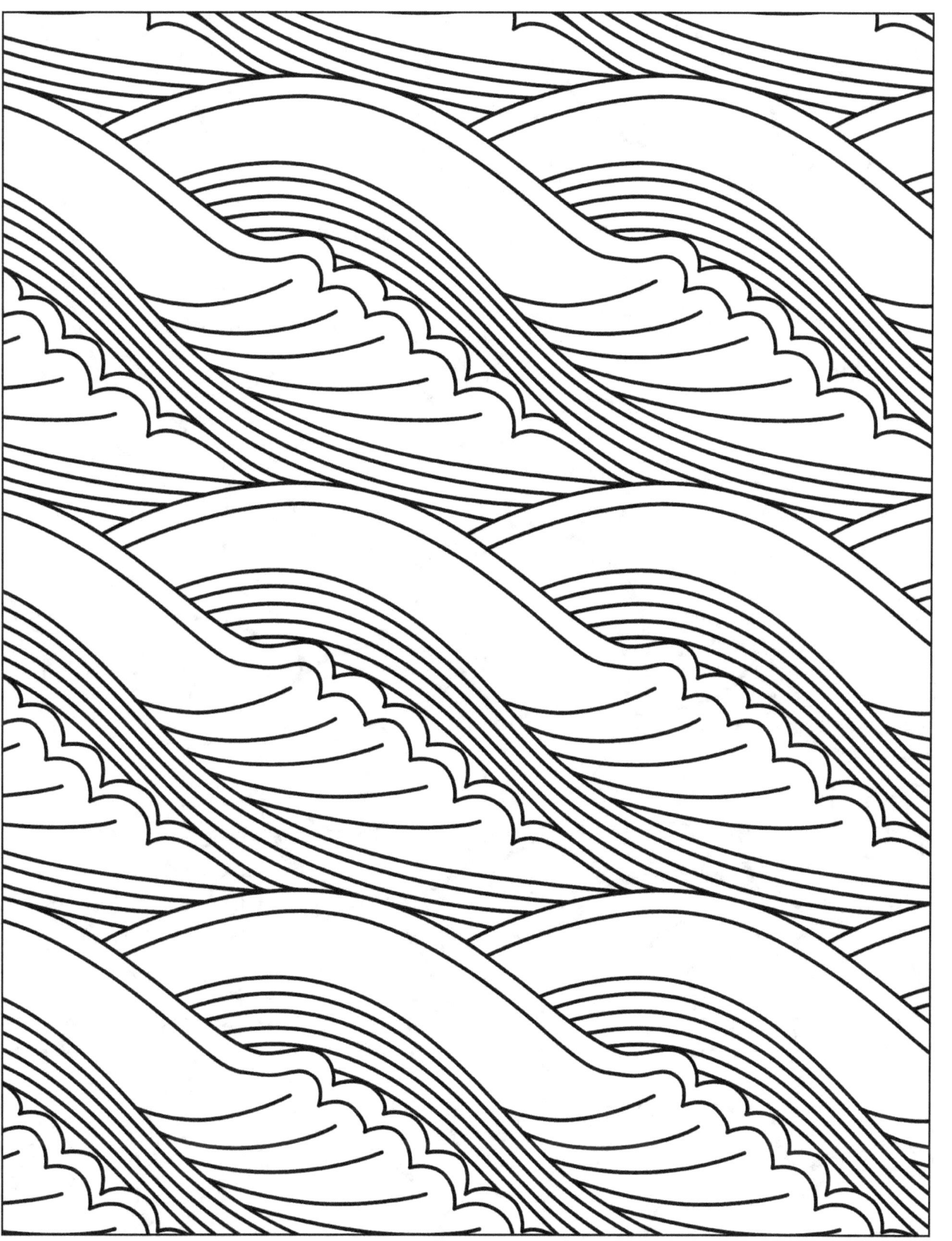

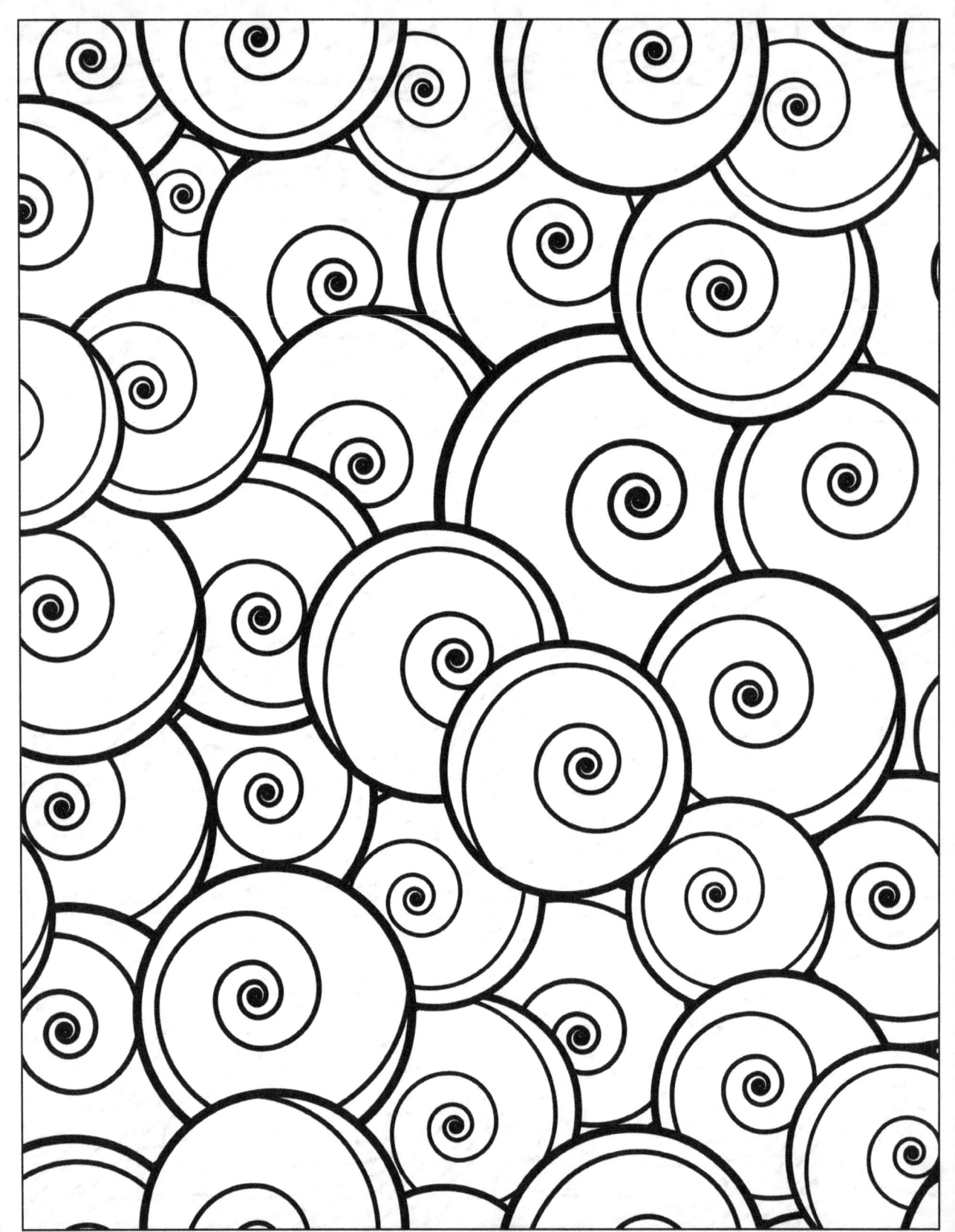

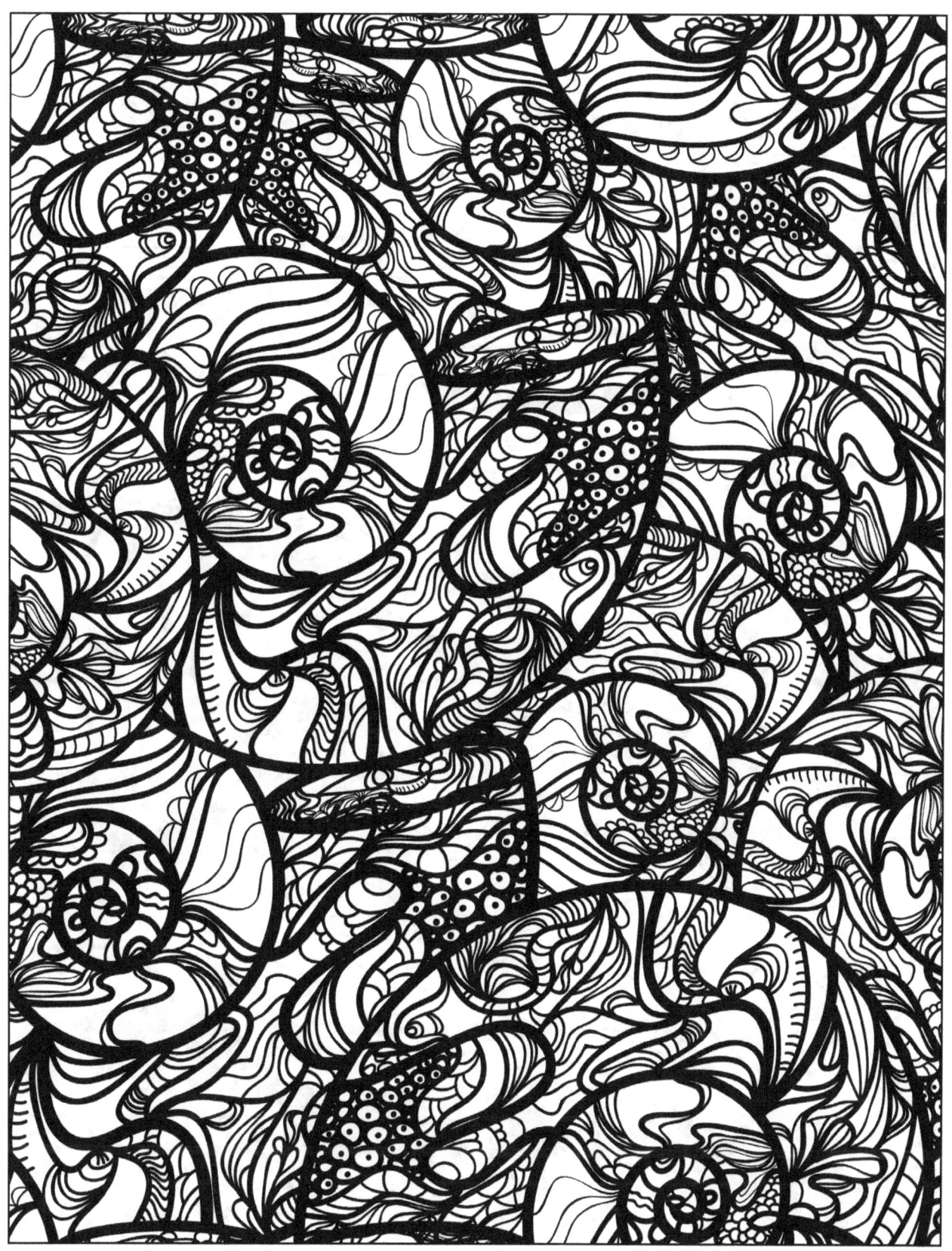

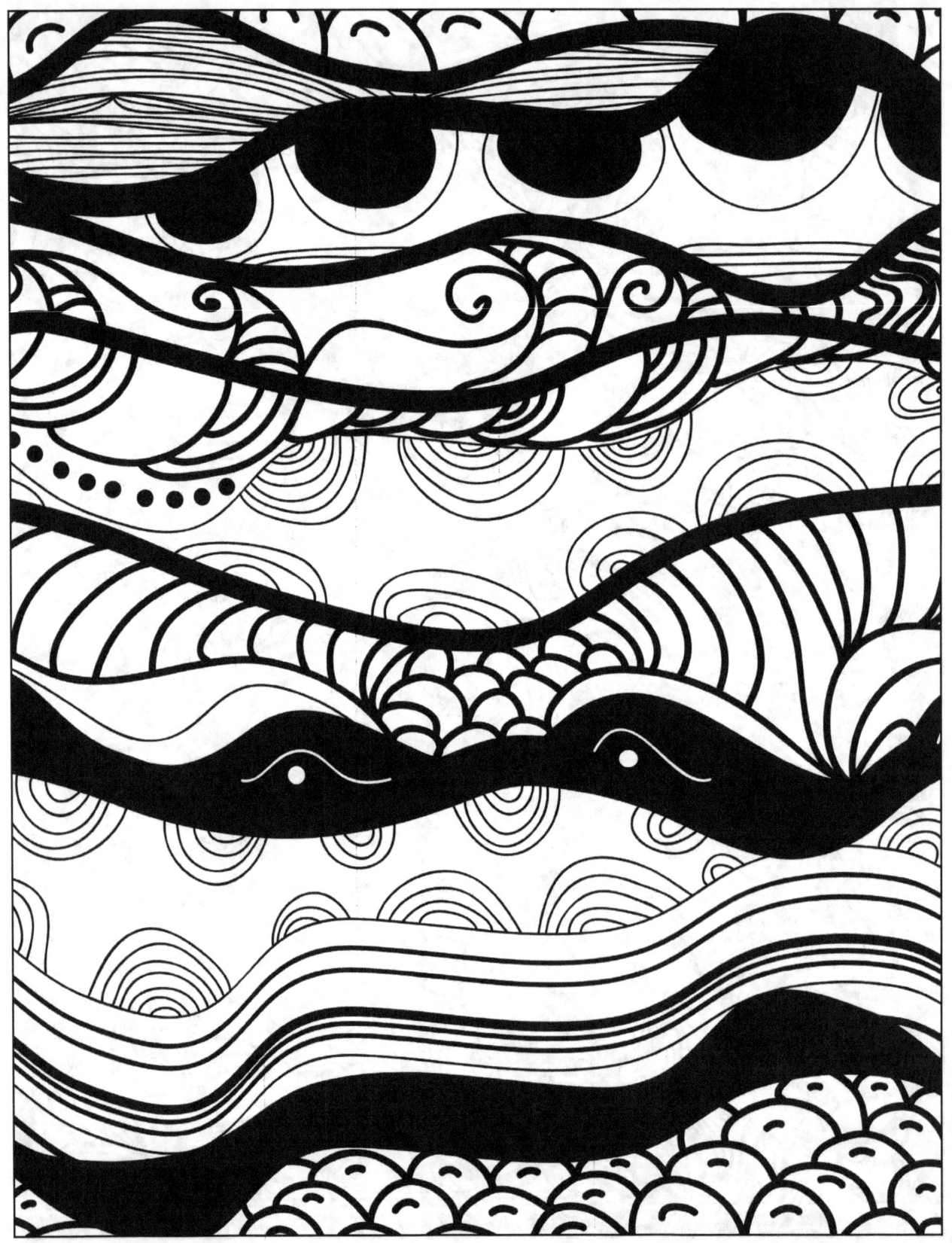

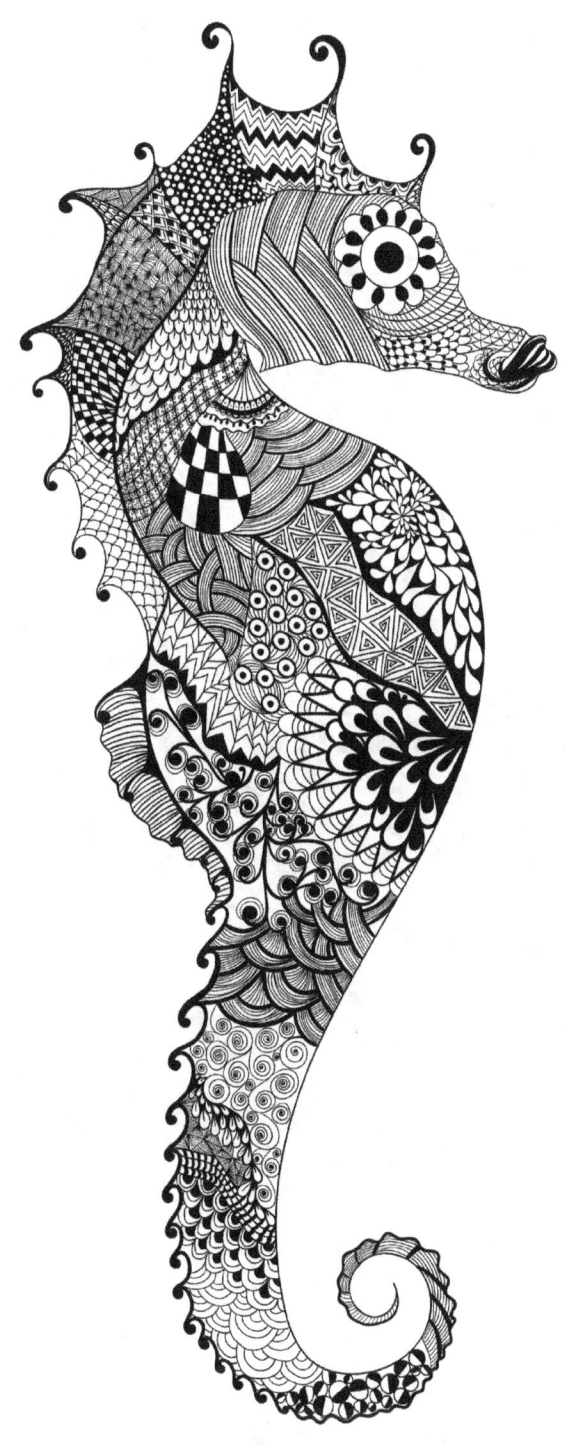

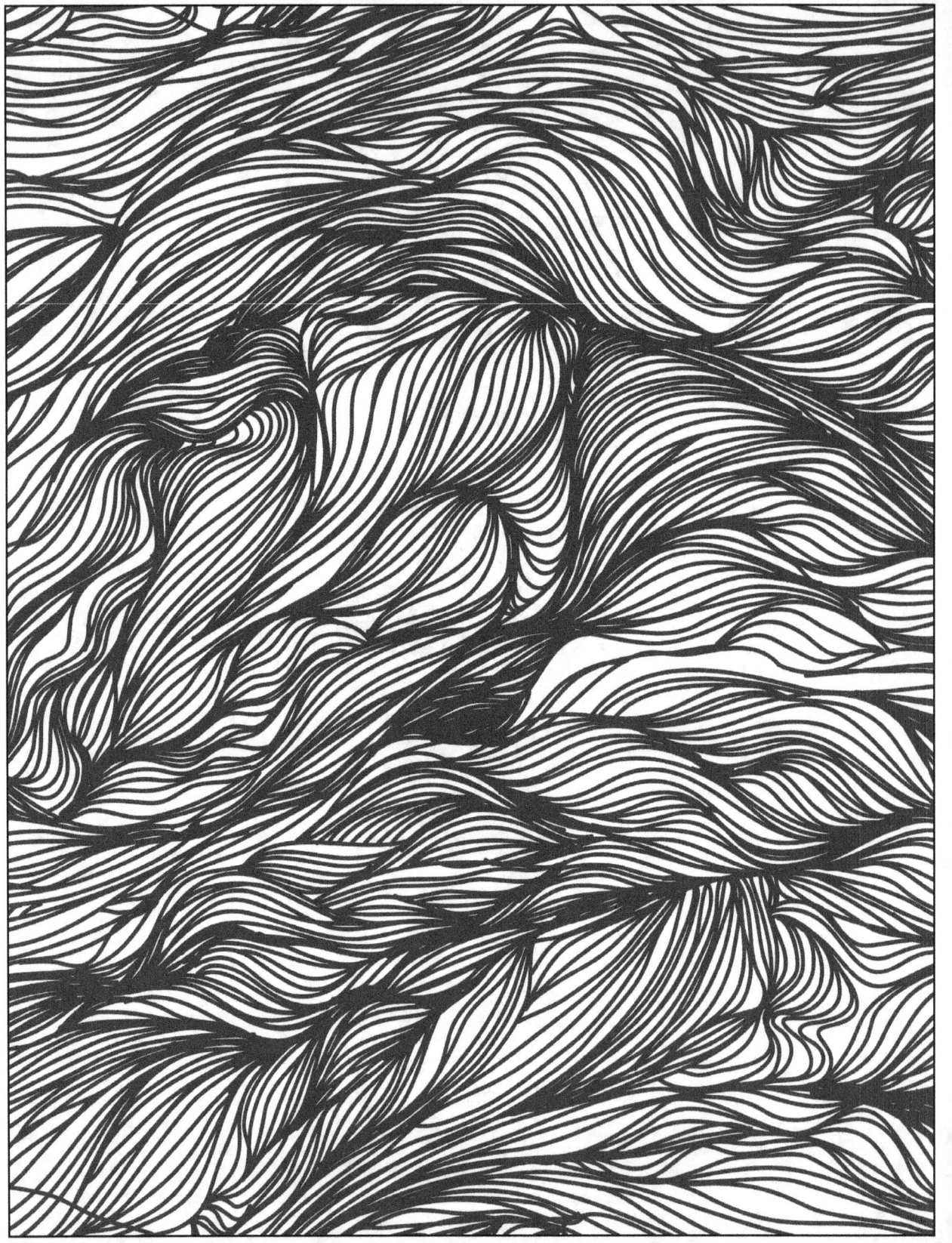

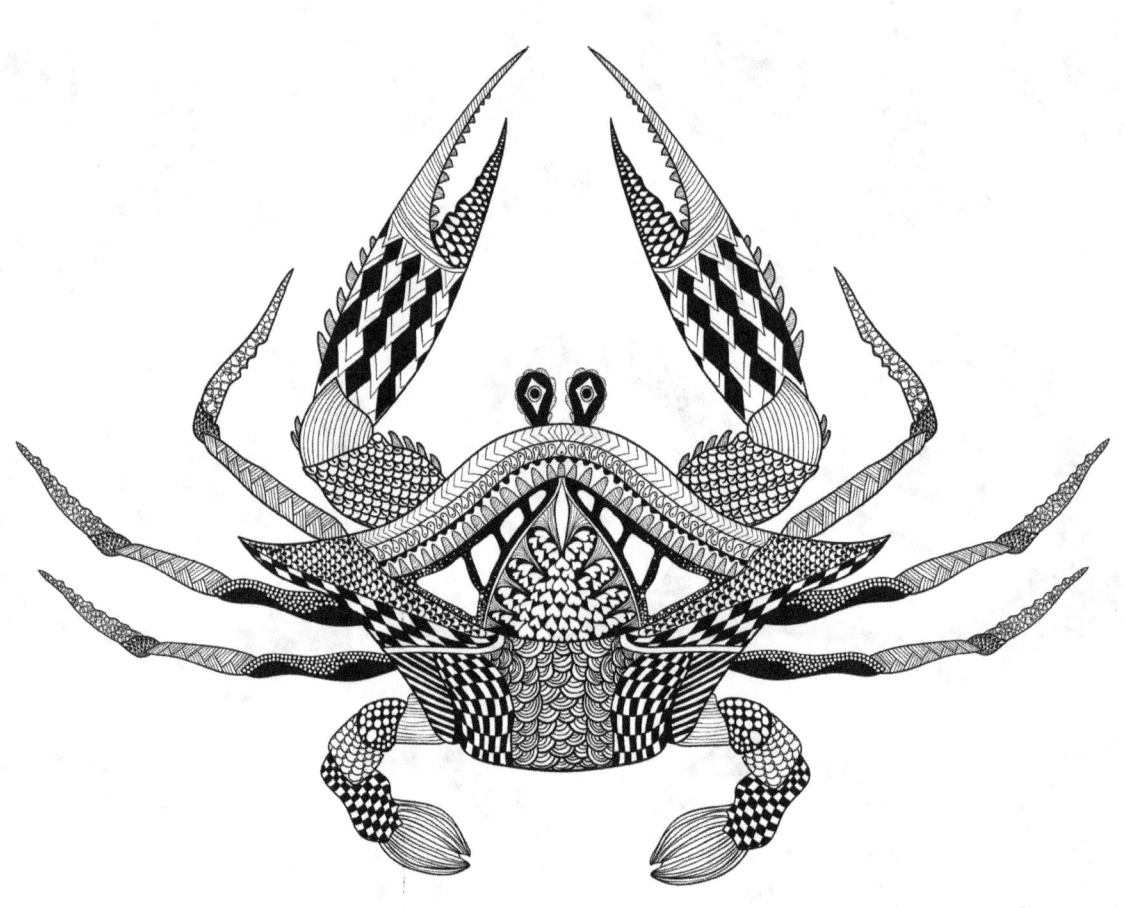

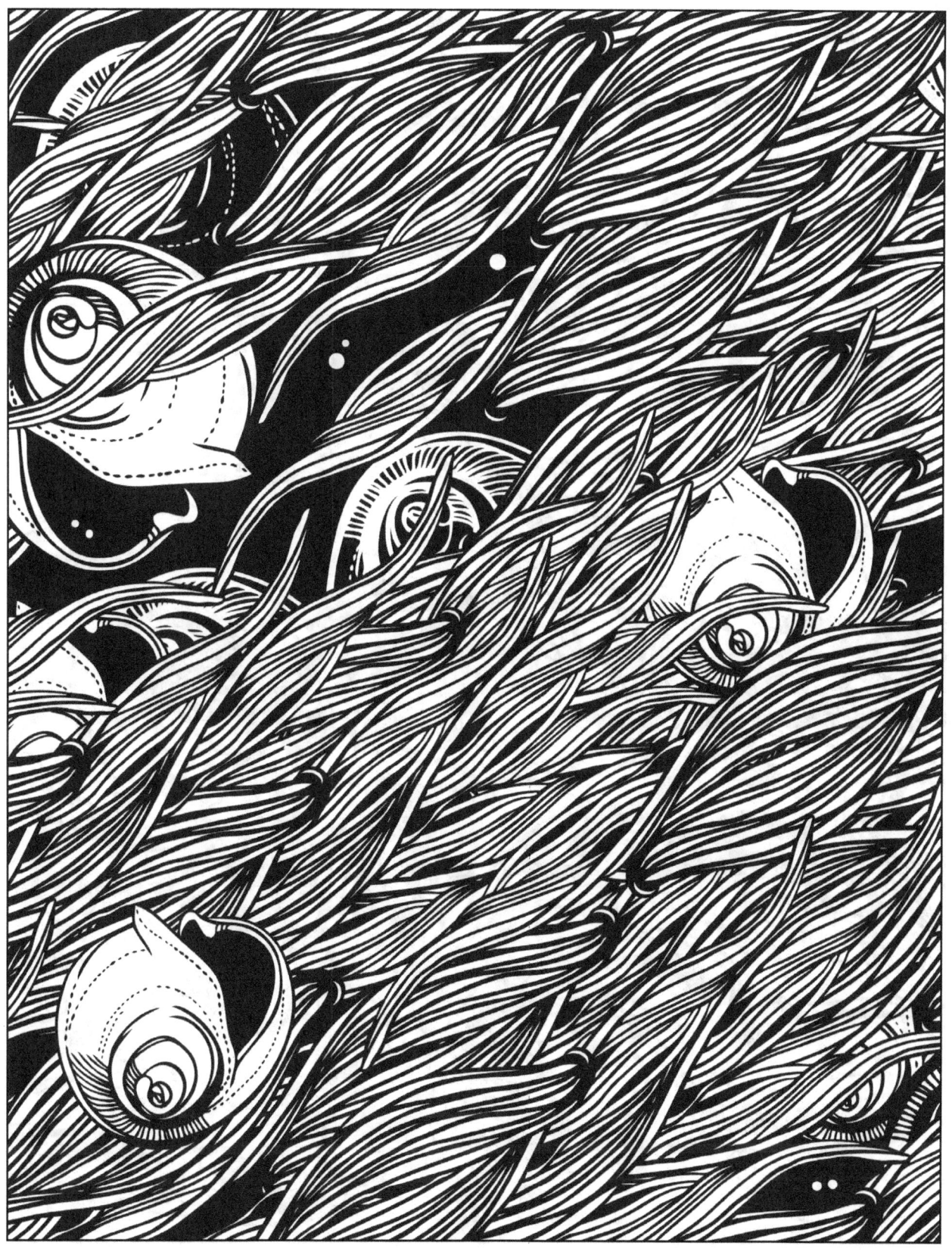

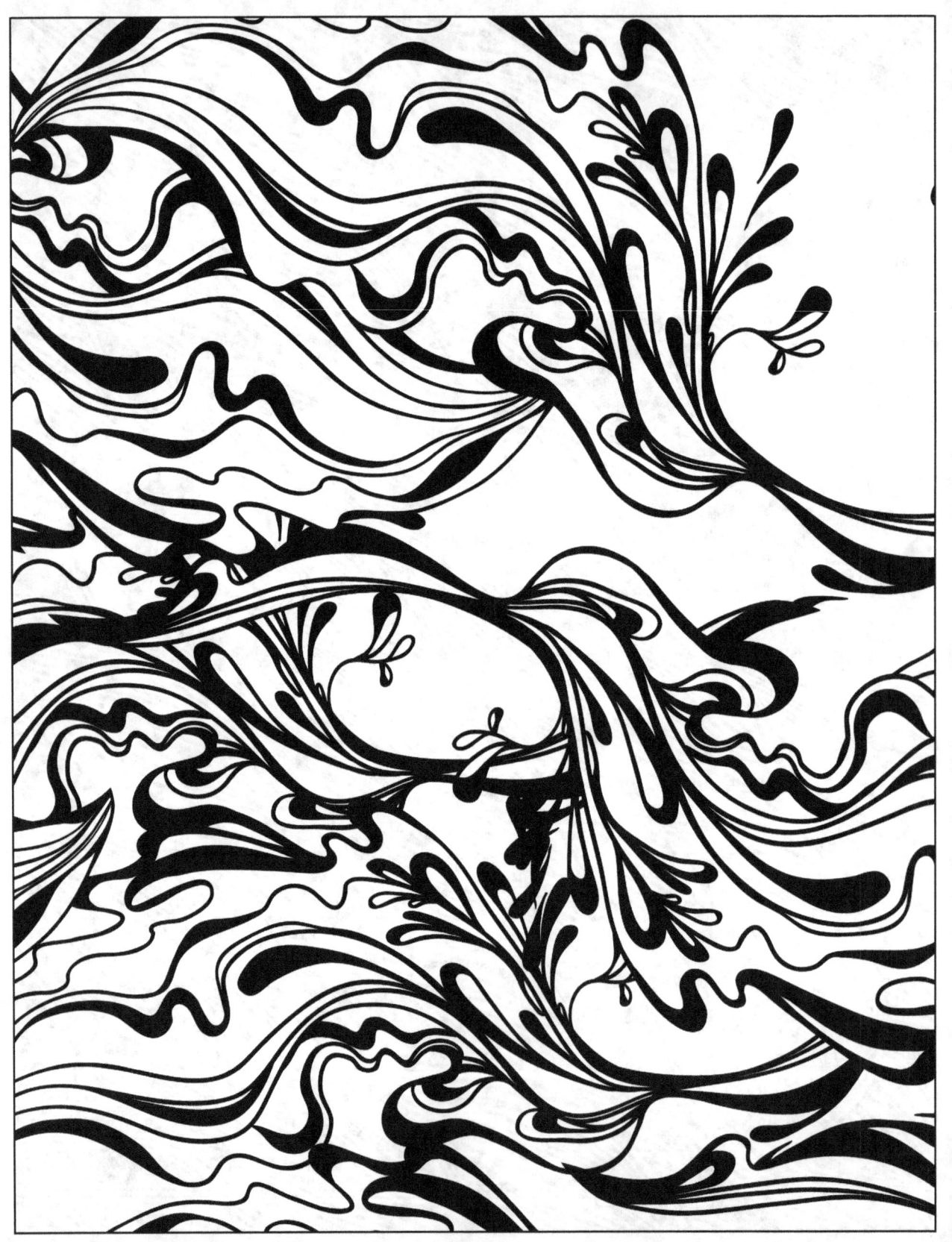

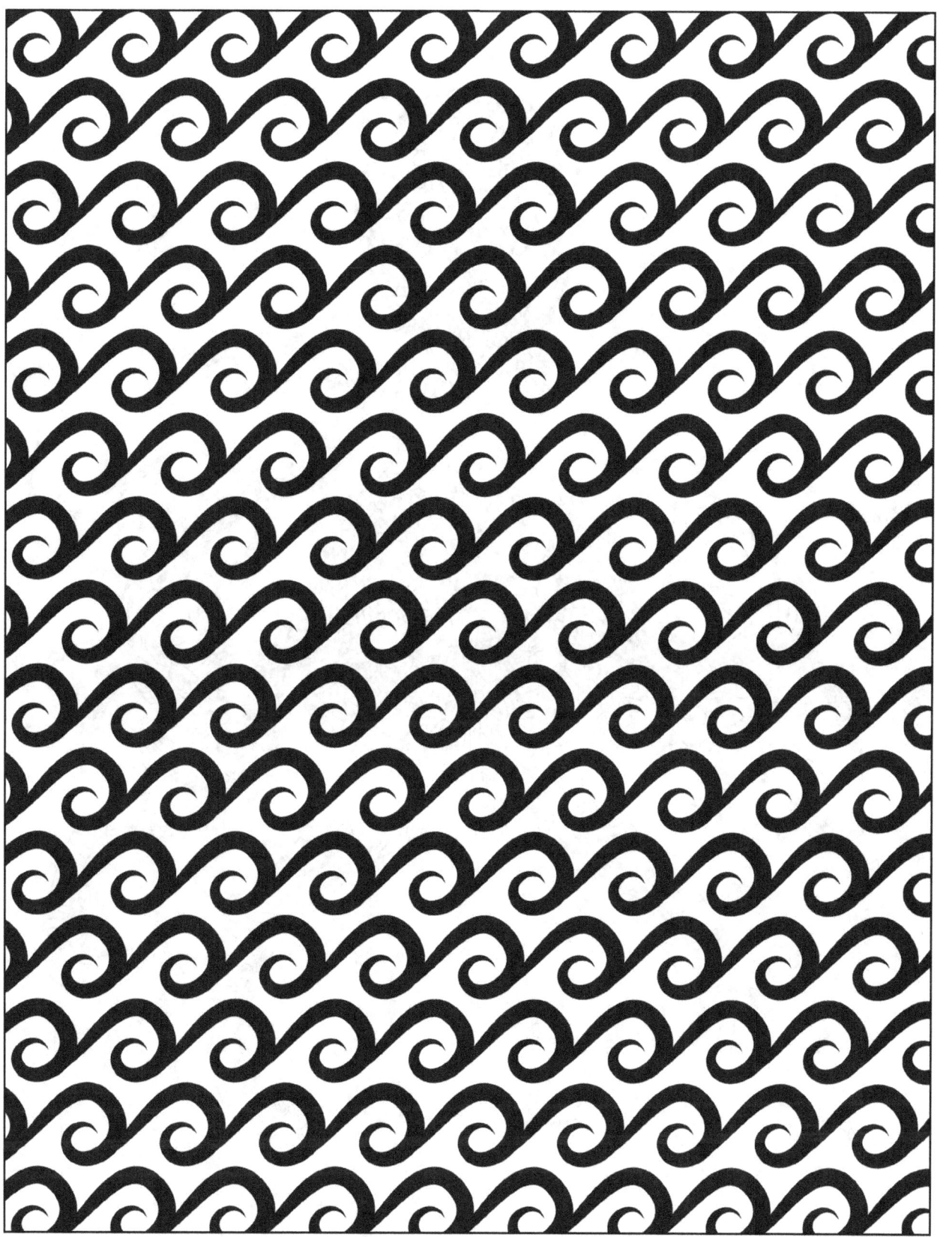

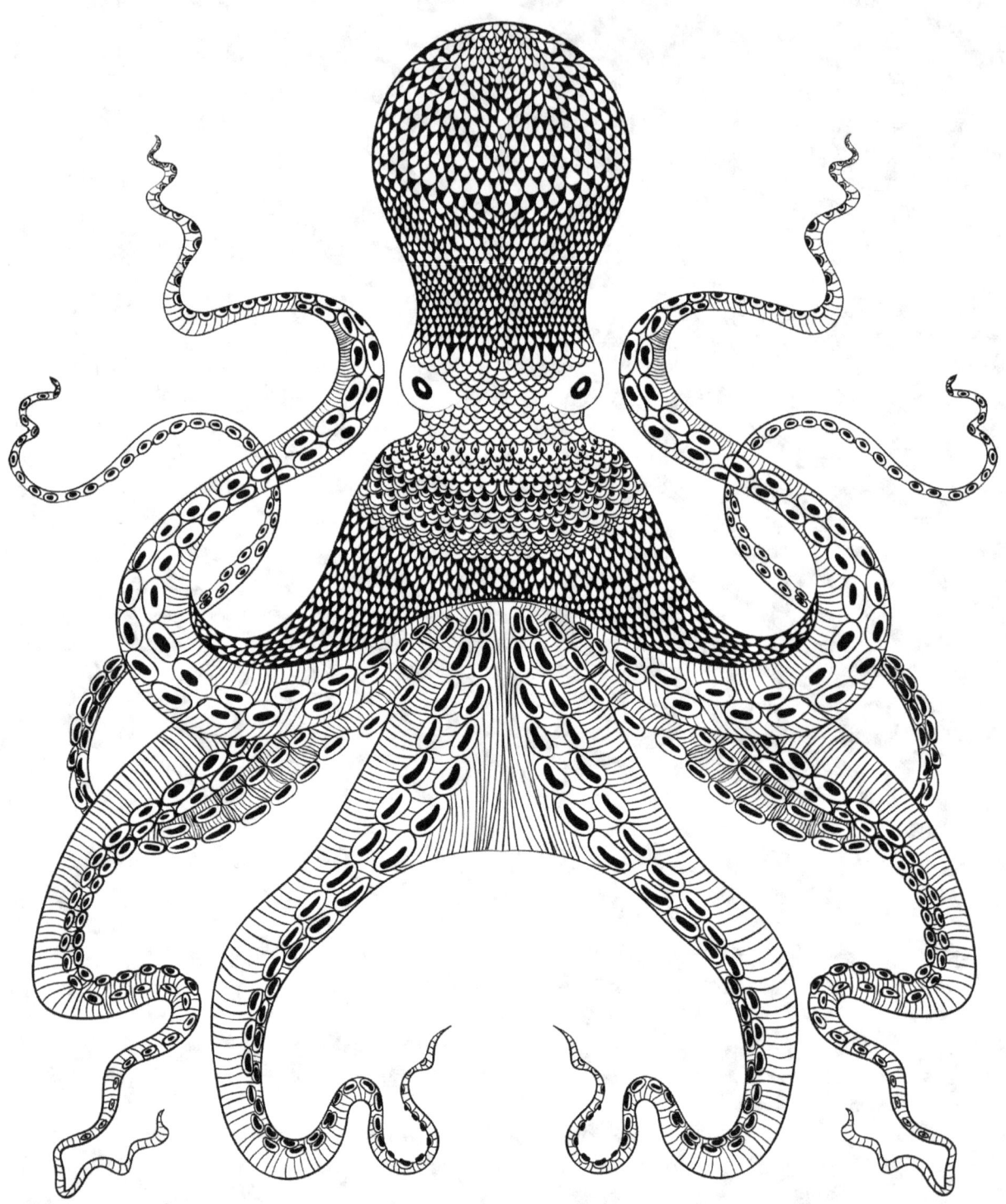

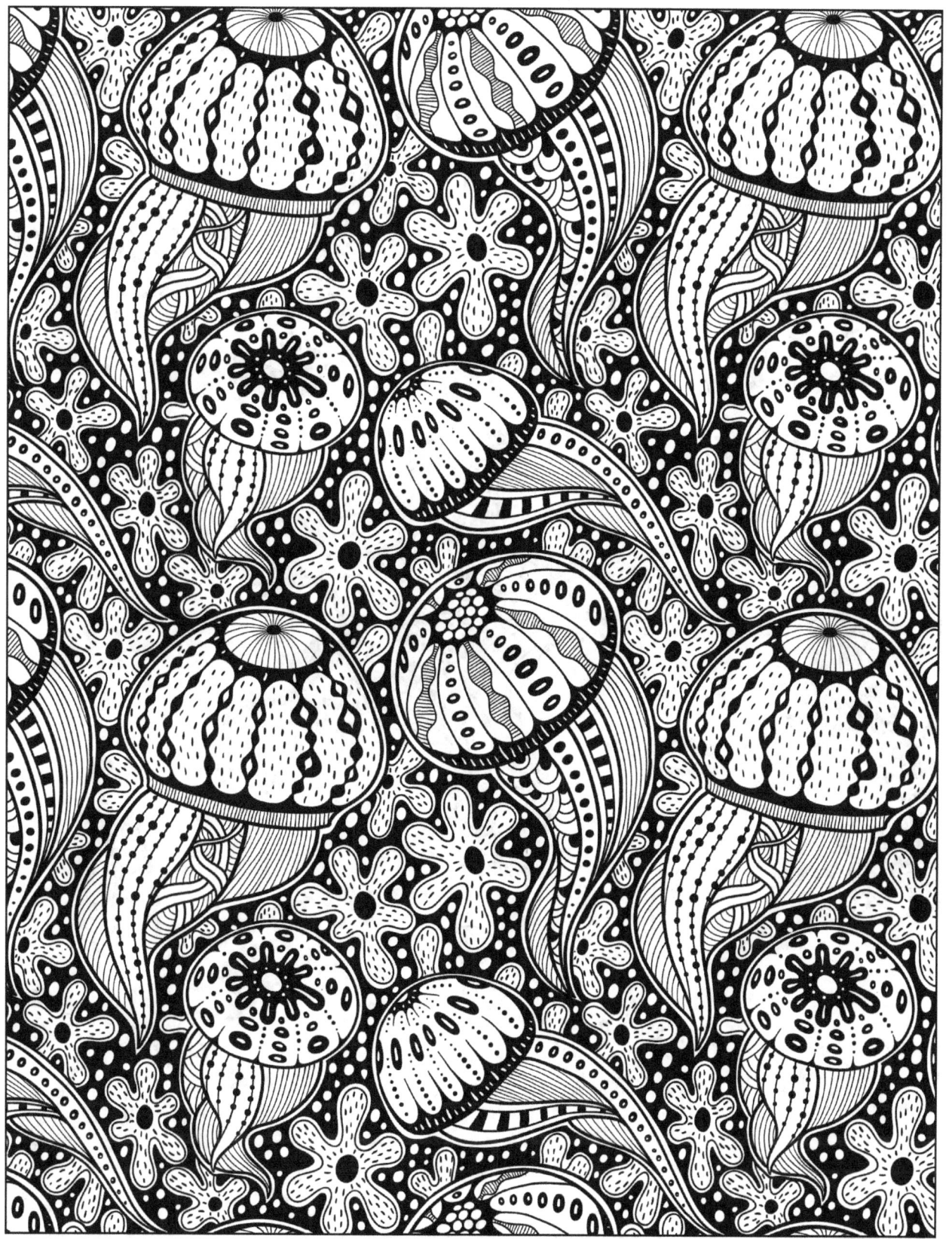

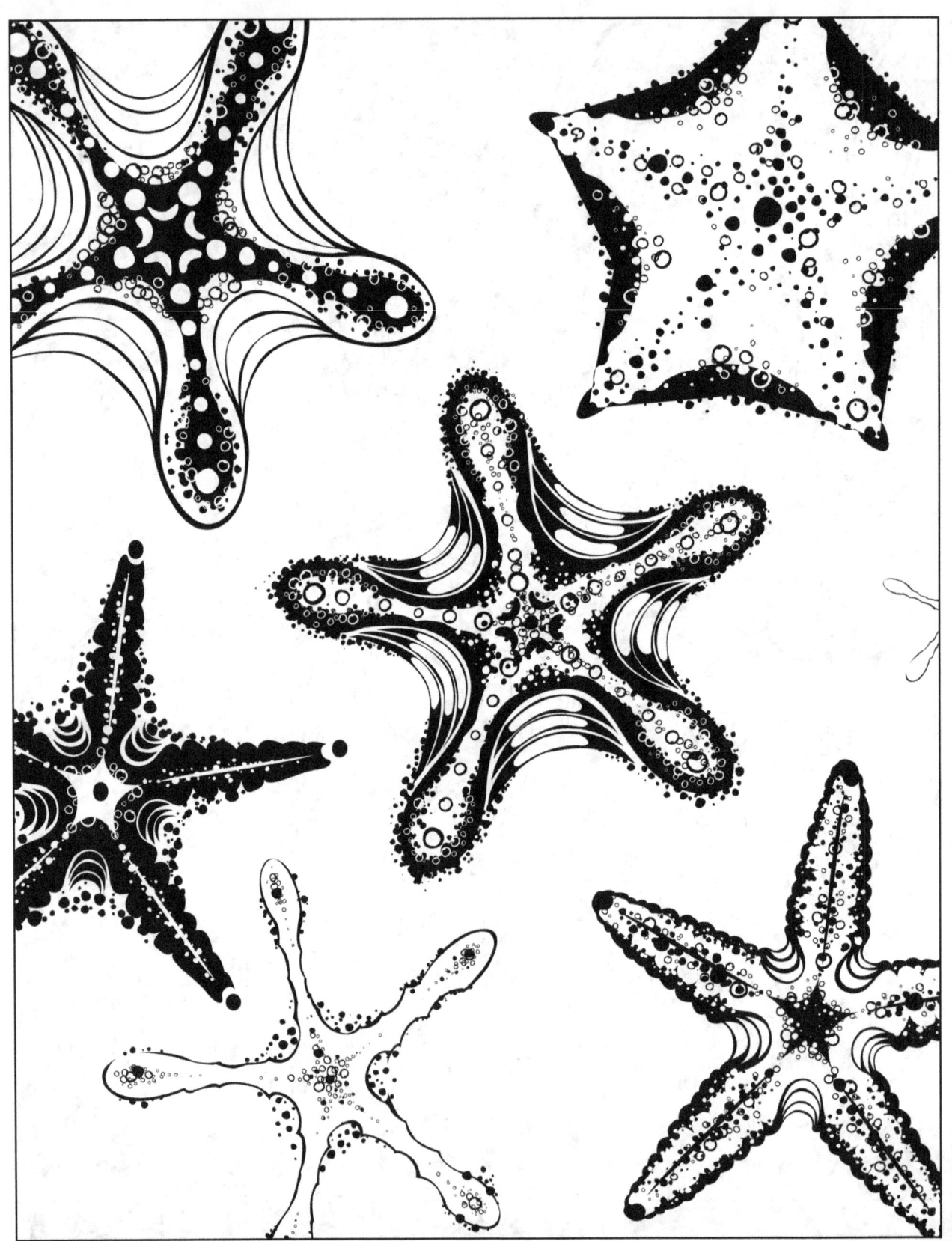

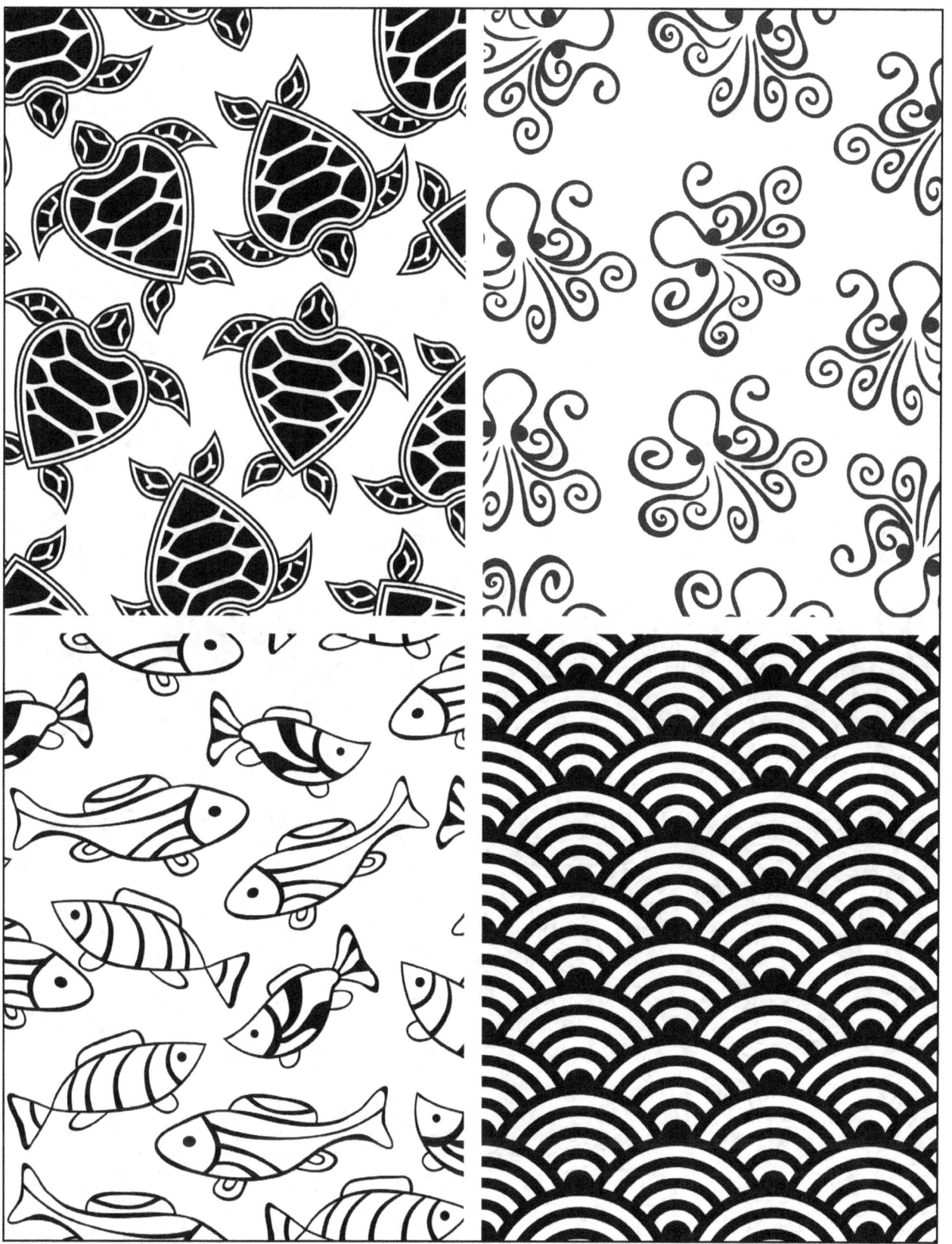

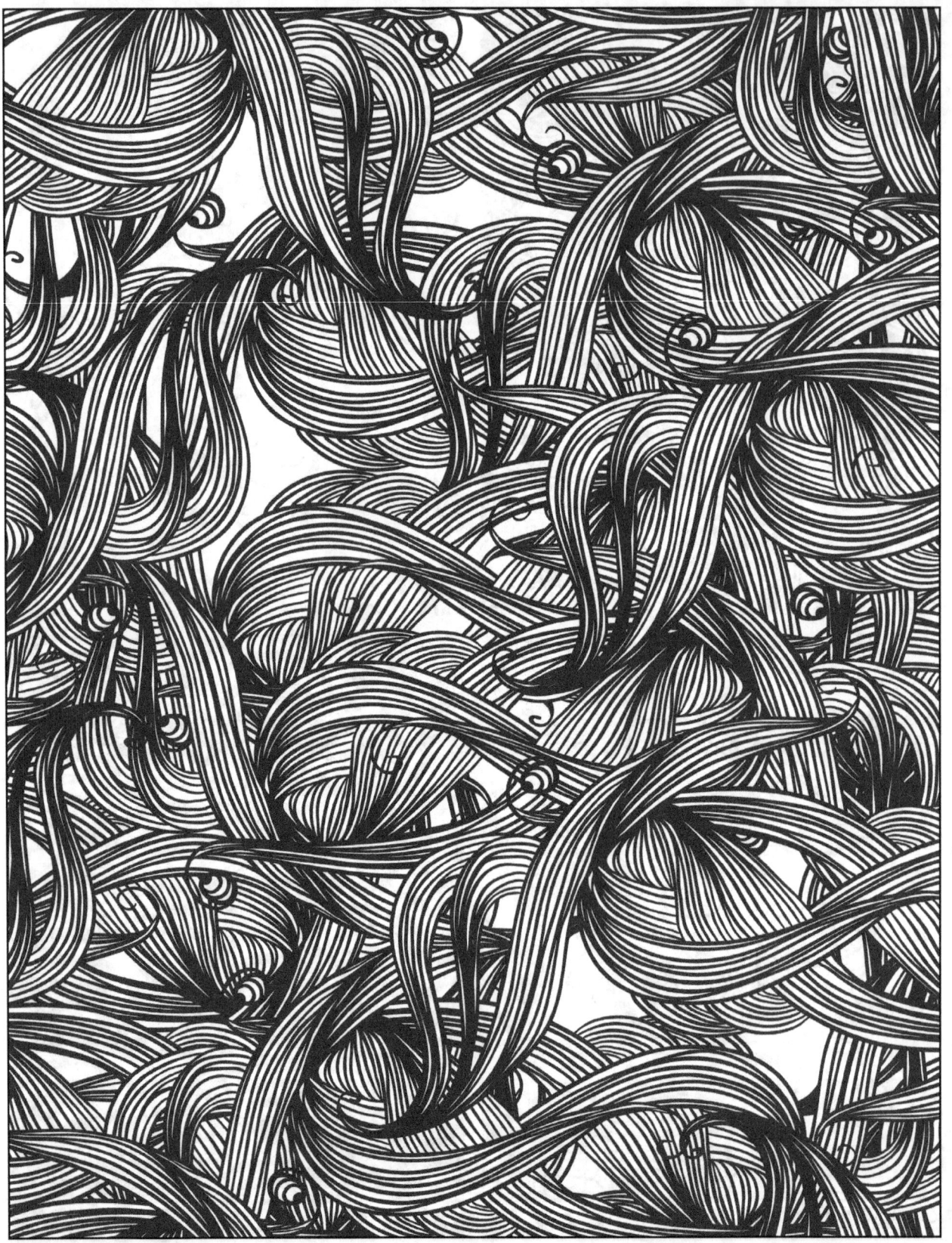

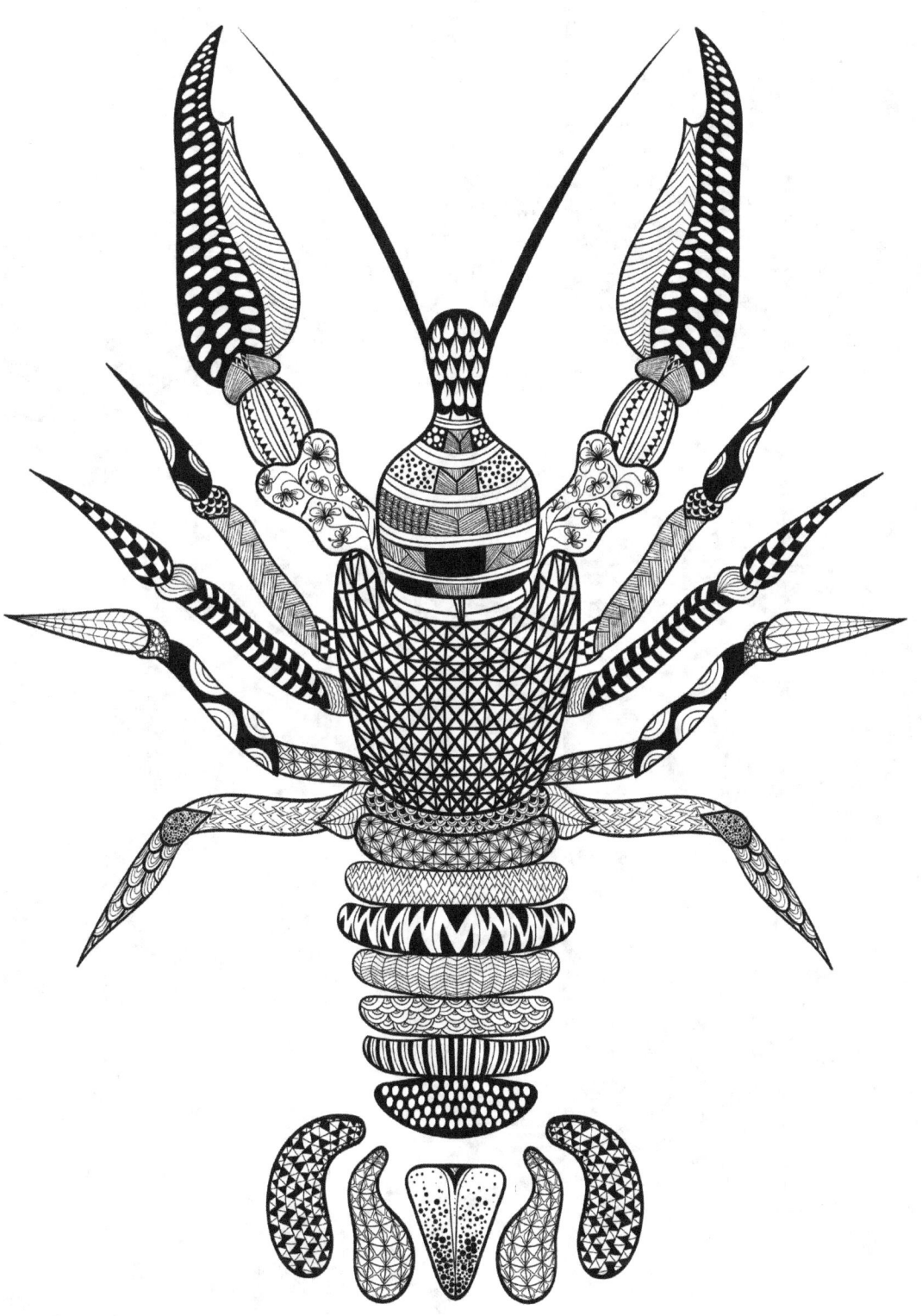

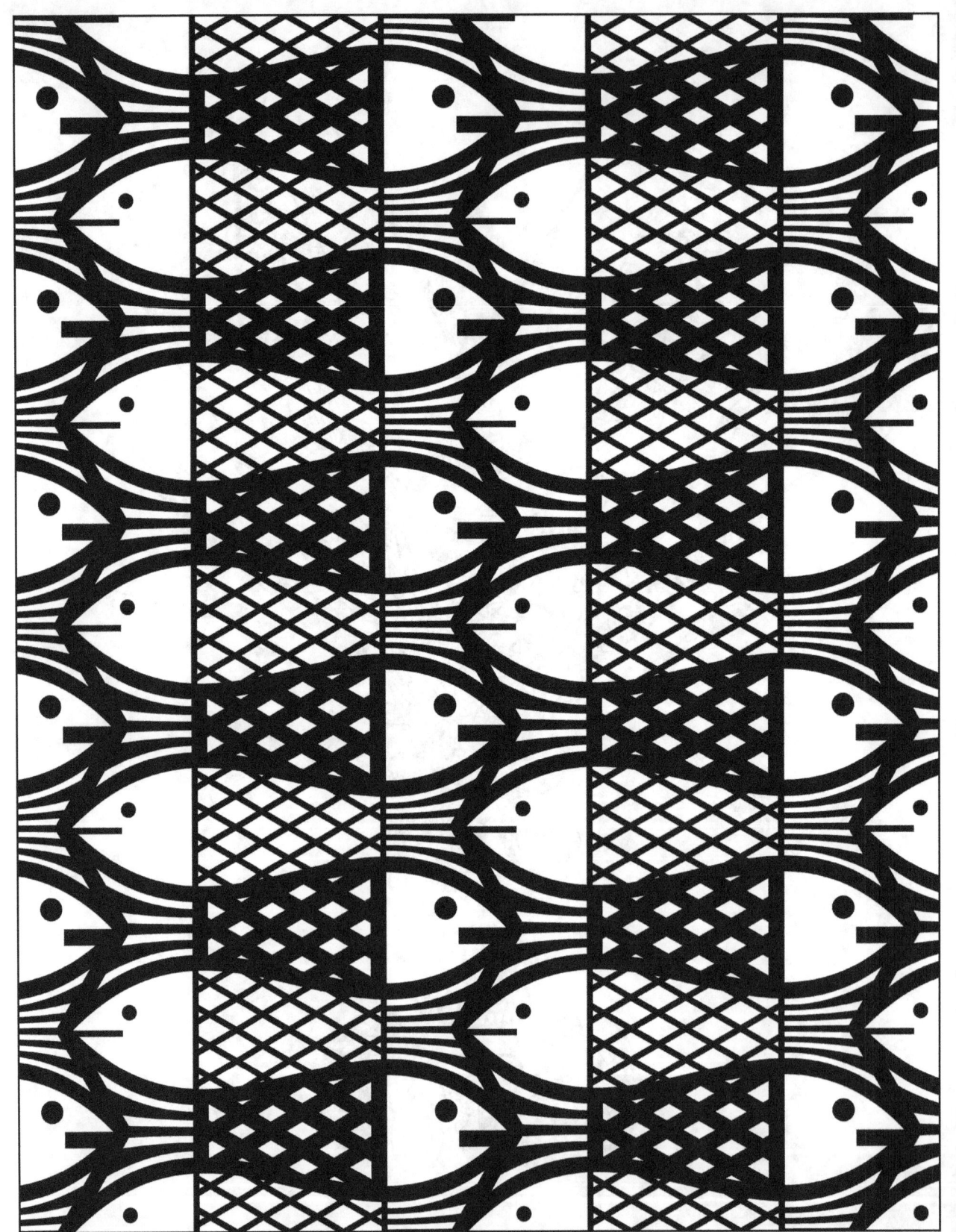

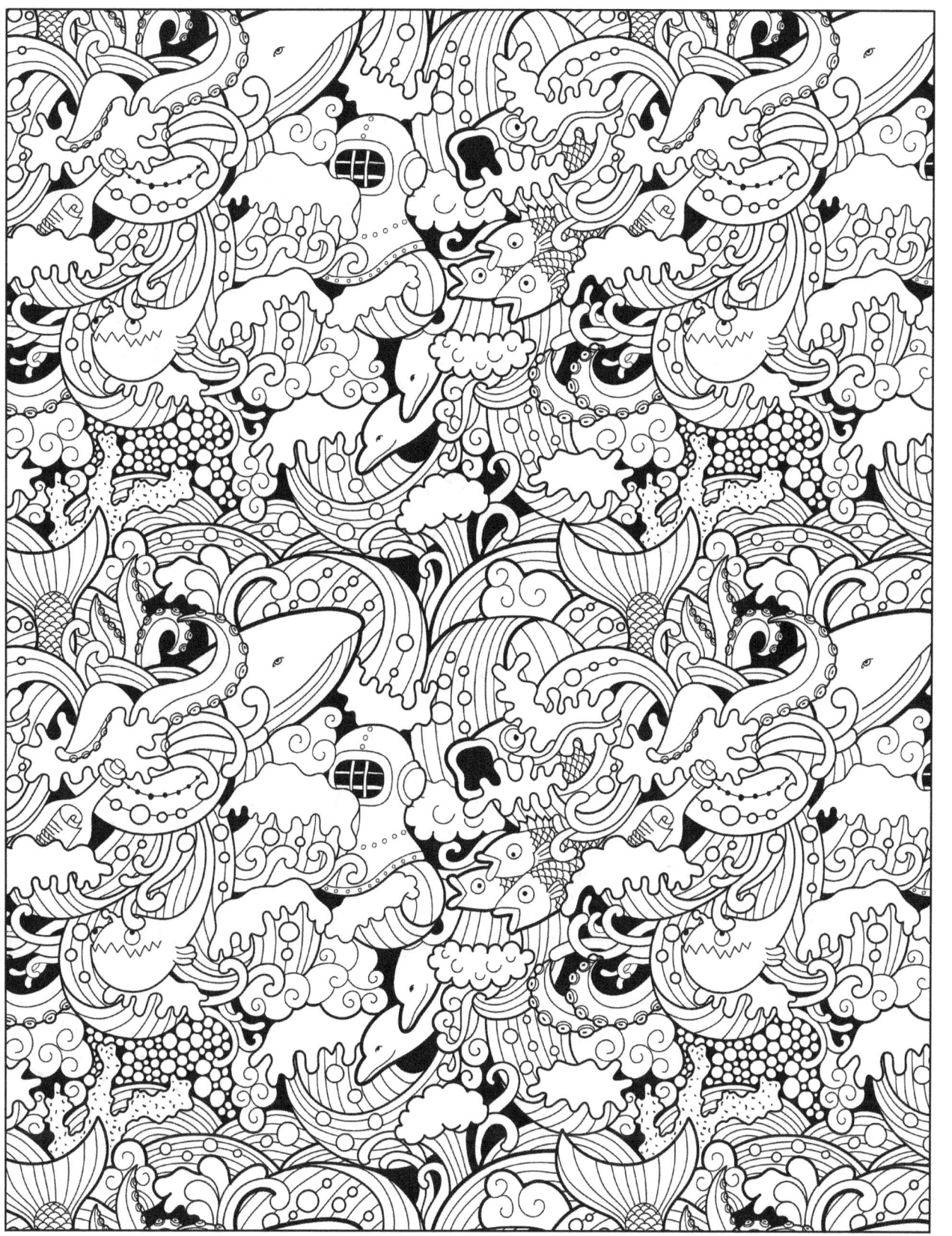

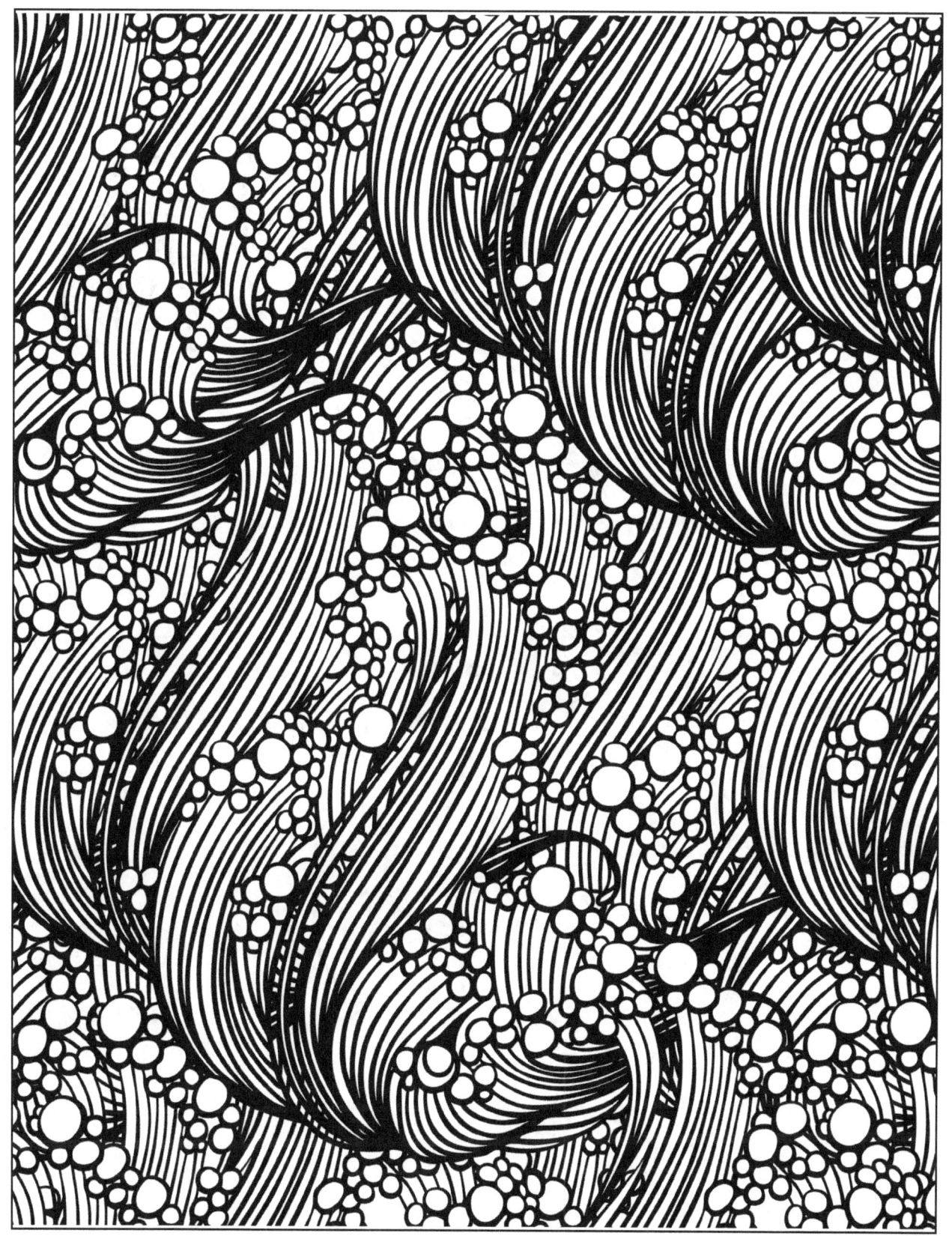

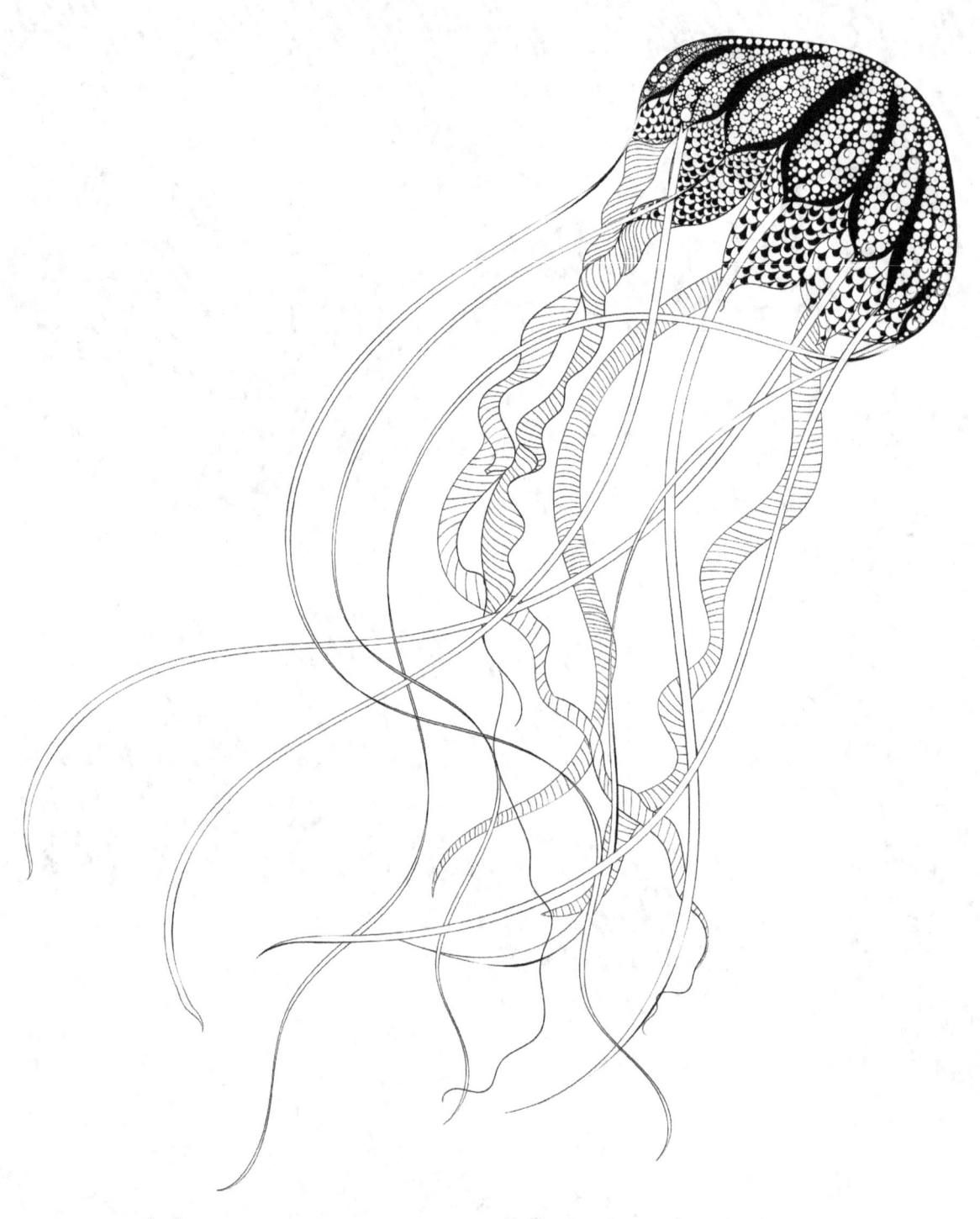

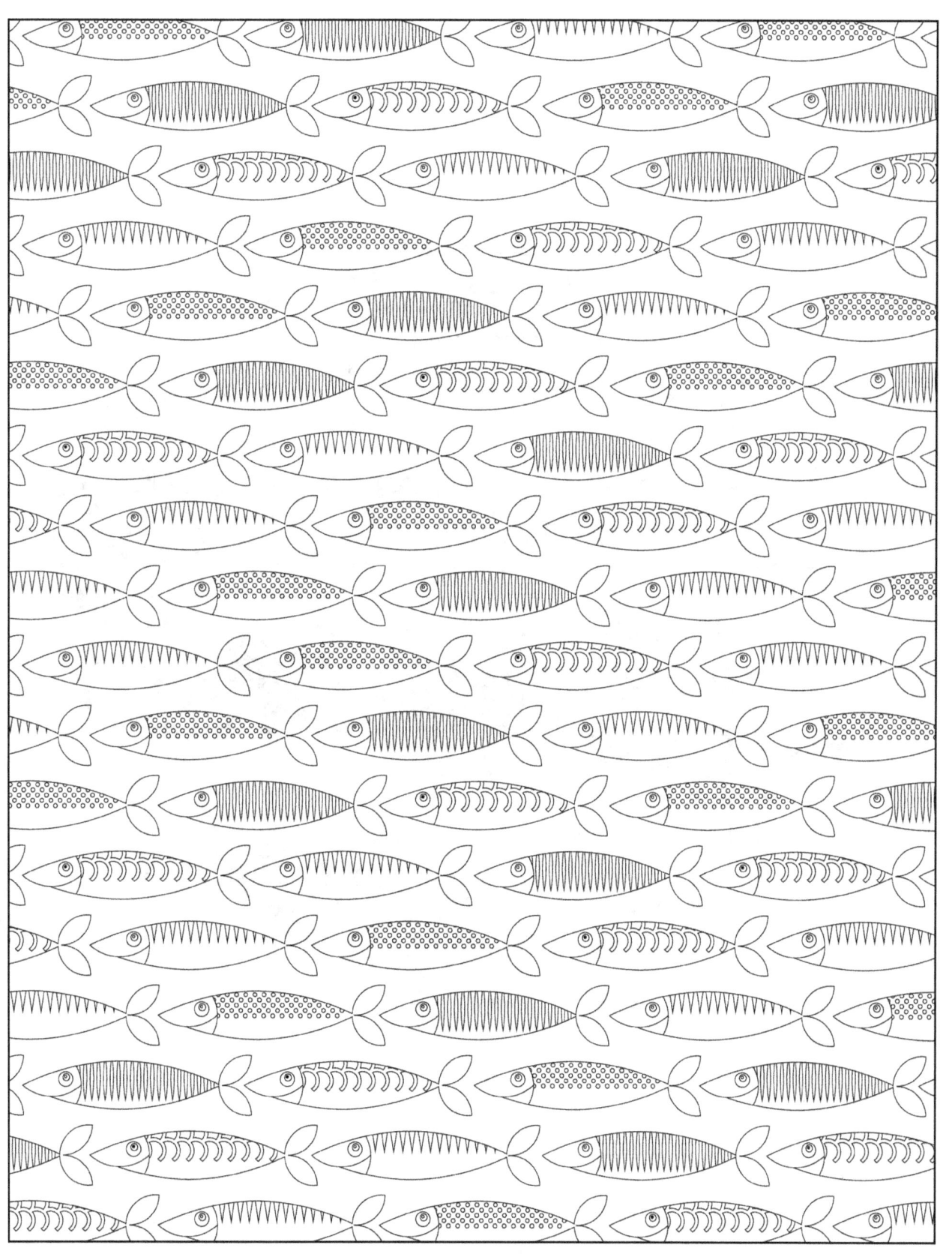

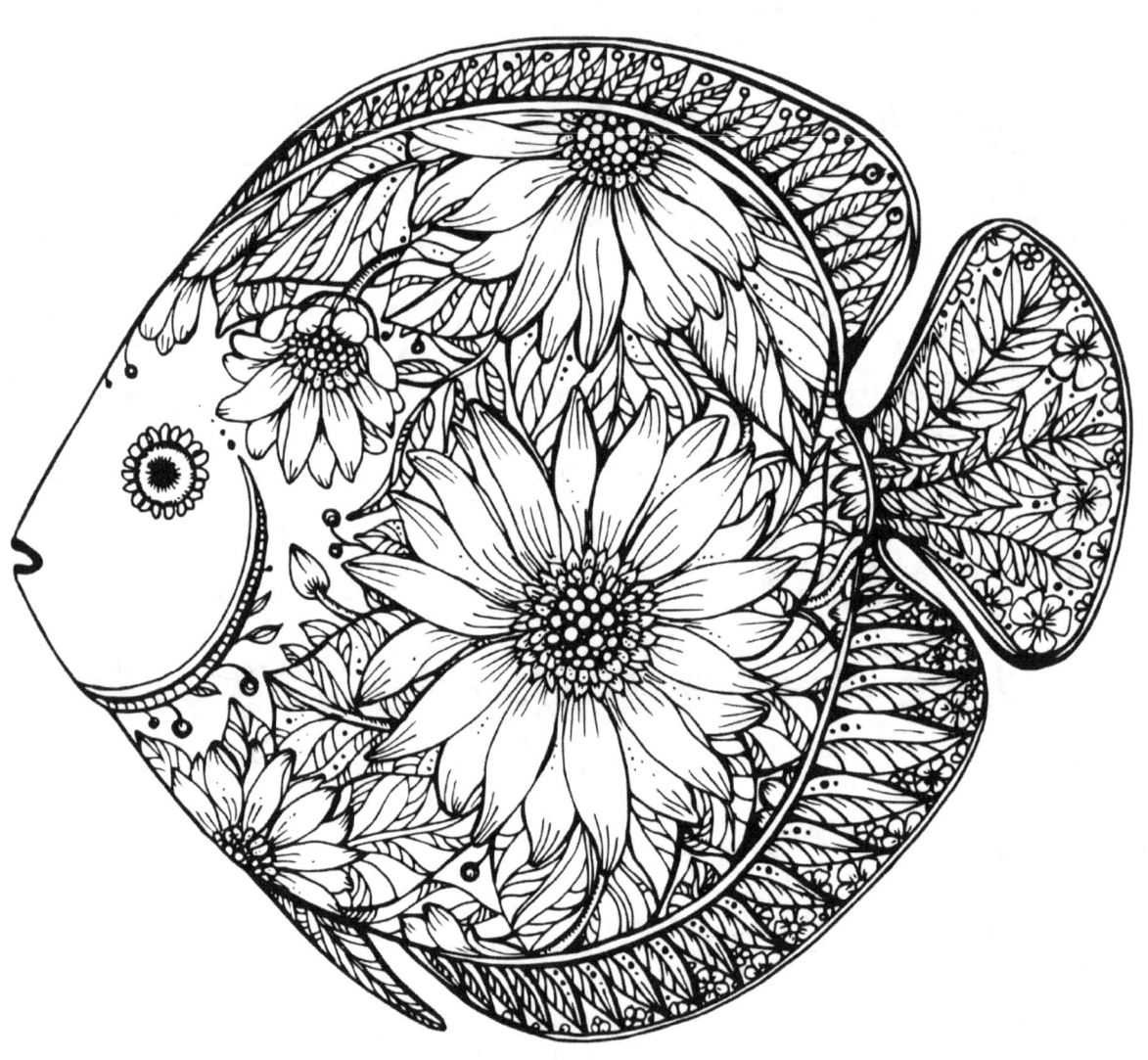

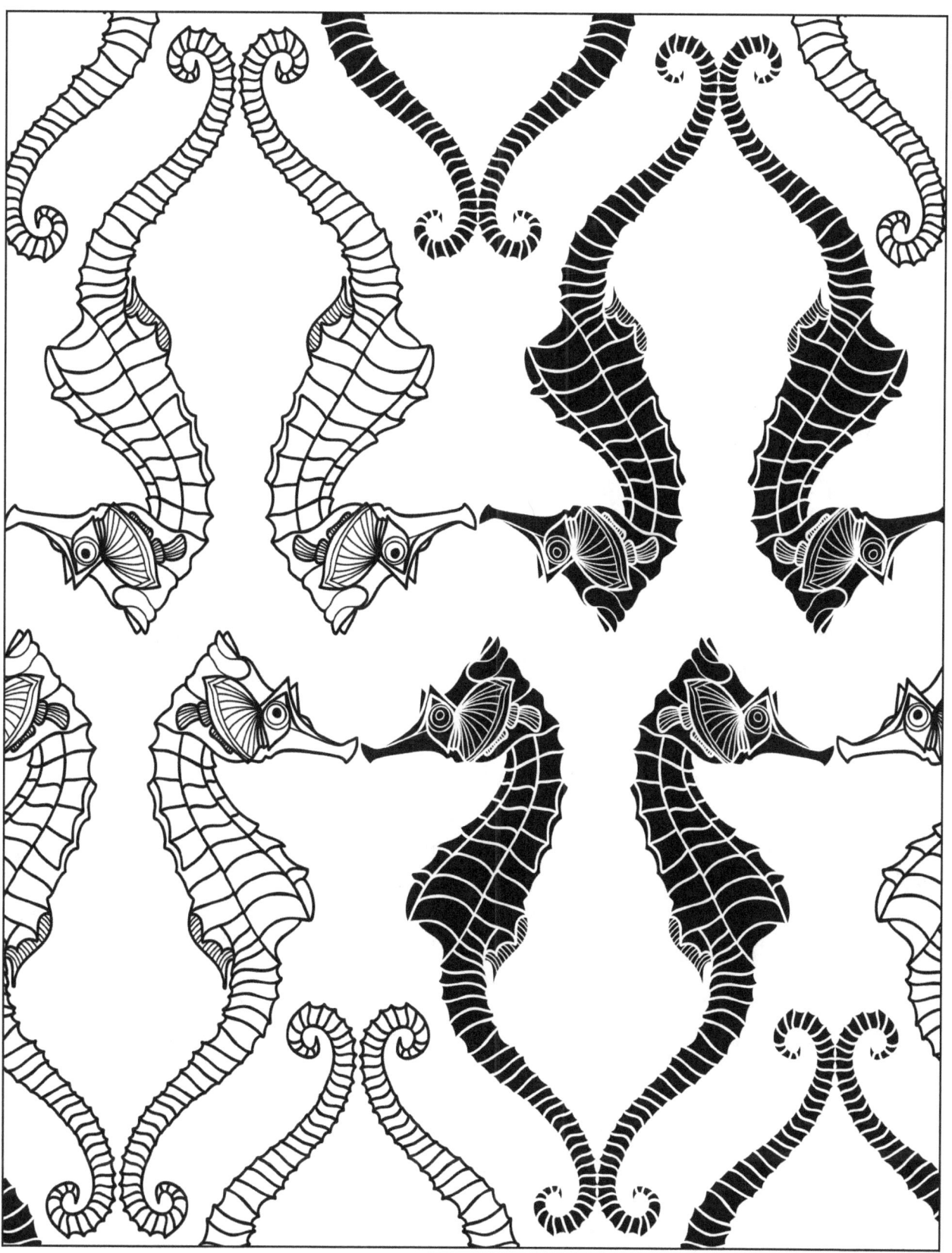

www.ingramcontent.com/pod-product-compliance
Lightning Source LLC
Chambersburg PA
CBHW081024170526
45158CB00010B/3152